GUN CULTURE USA

Where It Comes From and Why It Won't Go Away

Toni Hart

Disclaimer: "Gun Culture USA" is not meant to be a classic history book.
It is an attempt to understand my own personal story. The history you will
find herein is my interpretation of events. The style of this book is intended to be
informal and conversational.

ISBN: 0692844007
ISBN 13: 9780692844007
Library of Congress Control Number: 2017901997
Antoinette Wellman,New York, NEW YORK

This book is dedicated to the memory of Mrs. Helen Fleming

TABLE OF CONTENTS

CHAPTER 1

RUN OUT OF TOWN

My father was a doctor in a small town in Minnesota after World War II. He was mentally ill and explosively violent. The people in our hometown were so afraid he would shoot someone, they formed a vigilante group and ran my family out of town.

Running people out of town is an age-old form of vigilantism, a type of social control, the way small-town mid-America deals with its sociopathic citizens. Sometimes an individual is deemed so dangerous to the body politic they are simply forced out. The vigilantism the people in my hometown used wasn't the vigilantism of the Ku Klux Klan and it wasn't the vigilantism of the Old West. It's what I call "single-instance vigilantism" or "run the psycho out of town before he opens fire." My father had a terrible temper. He could start a fight in an empty room. He was born violent. His father was like that; I think it was genetic. My father would go into what I call "rage state." Something would trigger him and he would fly into a vicious rage, as if he were possessed. Once in rage state, there was no reaching him. Over time, he fought with everyone he considered an authority, his father, the police, the mayor, landlords, my mother's family. He became locked into a fantasy of revenge for crimes against him no one had committed. He was completely out of control.

The people in our hometown, Lake City, Minnesota, had grown up with my father and had been dealing with him for years. They had dealt with his rage and when he returned from college and the Army more violent than ever, they organized. The way my hometown ran us out is considered vigilantism for two reasons: it was a core group of men who did the strategizing and it was secret. Vigilantism is secret because it's a form of terrorism. That's why it works.

They used two methods to run us out: they organized a boycott of my father's medical practice and they tore down a house he was having built. It took them three years until my father finally gave up and left. He did not want to go. In those three years, because my father fought with every landlord, we were forced to move six times until there was nowhere else in Lake City to live. We were broke and homeless. My father took a salaried position as a physician on an Army hospital base in Iowa and we left town.

I was seven years old when we left and I didn't understand what was going on. I knew there was something terrible happening but I didn't know what it was. I never saw my paternal grandparents or my cousins again. What my father had done was so shameful they disowned us. No one ever spoke about it. It was a secret. My mother died when I was 14. To show you what kind of man my father was, when my mother was dying of cancer, her mother came to visit her, and my father threw my grandmother out. Soon after Mother died, my grandmother died and left me some money. I dropped out of high school, got an early admission to college, graduated and moved to New York City to live with my mother's sister. All my mother's sister would tell me about my father was, "Your father murdered your mother." She was so angry that was all she could say. I had no way of finding out what had happened to me as a child. There was a huge hole in my life I didn't understand.

I've spent most of my life trying to figure it all out. With the help of a psychiatrist and good friends and finally, my father's sister, I've been able to piece parts of the story together. I only learned about the vigilantism in 2007, when my father's sister was dying and told me the truth. Now I have a basic understanding of the kind of man my father was. But I was actually the victim of vigilantism in the middle of the 20th century. How that could have happened was incomprehensible to me. I began to research vigilantism and gun culture, a search that took me ten years and resulted in this book. I want to emphasize that this was a personal quest, and the gun culture I came to understand is the gun culture of the Midwest.

Now I live in New York City. When I told a friend back in Iowa that I was writing this story, he said to me, "Toni. Everyone in the Midwest will have heard a story like this. No one in New York will have any idea what you're talking about." And they don't. I am always asked by New Yorkers if I've ever shot a gun, but the way they ask me is, "HAVE YOU EVER SHOT A GUN?", like I get up in the morning and draw a bead on Bambi. I answer, "Yes, of course I've shot a gun, you silly liberal. I am a Midwesterner." I shot skeet, I shot branches off trees and I lined tin cans up along a fence and I shot those tin cans dead. It was loud and boring and I went off looking for something interesting to do. I do not like guns. When I killed those tin cans, I used a rifle. Farmers in my home states of Minnesota and Iowa have rifles to keep the foxes out of the henhouse. On a farm, you have to be able to protect your animals, so rifles are common in the Midwest. Their long barrel and the rifling inside the barrel means you have accuracy at a great distance, which is perfect for a farm. Many people also had shotguns. No one I knew had a handgun. Most of my Midwestern friends who lived in town had a rifle in the house, probably one that had been used for hunting. Now, it was up on a shelf in a dusty closet and its existence was forgotten. It was there because every man in the Midwest thinks that some day, he will go duck hunting.

This familiarity with guns in small-town America is the opposite of the situation in New York City. Most New Yorkers I know who grew up in the city are from families who migrated from Europe directly to New York. There is no gun culture in Europe. Europe was settled by, I don't know, the Huns, a couple thousand years ago, and they probably threw rocks at each other. America was settled a couple hundred years ago. It was a horribly violent country in the early days, and if you didn't have a gun, you were in trouble. Not one of my New York–born friends has ever used a gun and none of them have anyone in their family history who was a gun owner. I don't know anyone in the Midwest who did not grow up with a gun in the house. In New York, I live in a protective cocoon. The building I live in has 24/7 doormen who are like pit bulls in uniform. There are video cameras on every entrance to my building and in the hallways. The other buildings, restaurants, bars, hotels and delis in my neighborhood all have video cameras recording everything that happens on the street. When you walk from one end of my block to the other, you've been on so many cameras you think you're a movie star. My precinct stationhouse is six or seven blocks away. I can have the police at my front door in five minutes. It is in New York City, of all places, that I feel safe. And what about living out in the countryside in Iowa? What about people who live a good half-hour away from police help? Read Truman Capote's *In Cold Blood* and tell me that you wouldn't want protection if you lived out in the country.

Since the shootings in Newtown, Connecticut and Orlando, Florida, many Americans are talking about gun culture and how to change it. Part of the problem with this issue is that liberals don't know what gun culture is. The difference in lifestyle between gun country and liberal cities is enormous. It's as if there were two Americas. If you want to change something as deeply ingrained in the American psyche as gun culture, you'd better know what you're talking about. Urban Americans don't understand how violent mid-America can be and they don't understand the history of violence in America. I grew up in gun country with a right-wing father, I was run out of town in a vigilante action and I ran away from my father and moved to New York City where I studied political science as a graduate student at Columbia University. If anyone can explain gun culture to liberals, it's me. Some of my best friends are liberals. I am going to tell you right now that you will not like some of the things I say. I am not defending gun culture. I am explaining it.

CHAPTER 2

WHY DOES AMERICA HAVE 310 MILLION GUNS?

Here's a statistic that stops my liberal friends cold. In America, until the early 1990s, the estimated number of guns was 200 million. Many of those were the old guns, the rifles and shotguns from the farming days. Now, the estimated number of guns in America is 310 million. What the hell happened here? 200 million guns to 310 million in 25 years? Remember, the gun culture I understand is the Midwestern gun culture, and in the Midwest, the hell that happened was methamphetamine.

Meth moved into Iowa in the 1980s, and in the 1990s, it exploded into power. Meth was everywhere, destroying lives, families, everything in its path. Entire towns became ghost towns when meth hit. It took over the state of Iowa. I don't think there has ever been such a powerful or instantly addictive drug. Meth not only induces violent behavior and paranoia, it lures a victim into the trap of invulnerability. That drug is magic – if you are the devil. It can take a person down in a very short period of time, and with that person goes their family, their friends and their business. Meth has inspired more violent crime than all the other drugs put together.

It is the drug of prison gangs and of skinheads. It is the drug of home invasions. You might remember a home invasion in 2007 in Connecticut. A doctor was injured and his wife and two daughters were raped, tortured and burned to death. That was a classic crystal meth crime. It has been estimated that in some states, meth is behind 70 percent of the property crimes. The drug is a font of cruelty. It can be heartbreaking to look at photos of homes that take in babies who are waiting for foster homes, having been taken from meth-addicted parents. There will be three or four nurses, each with two babies, one in each arm and sometimes a third child on their lap. In small-town Midwestern hospitals, police departments have had to post cops in the emergency rooms on Friday and Saturday nights. Somebody would get into a meth fight, end up in the hospital, his buddies would come in to protect him, the opposing gang would come in and there would be a shoot-out in the ER.

As drug use and its resulting crime grows, people are arming. The plague of methamphetamine radically changed the guns Midwesterners wanted. It was meth that brought the handguns and the semi-automatic assault rifles. Those rifles were developed in the Vietnam War. In the 1970s, they were not a particularly popular gun but when the violence of meth hit the Midwest, the assault rifles came into high demand. People were terrified. They wanted big semi-automatic guns that could be used against a rampaging meth gang. Regular rifles are single-shot guns that were deemed useless against drugs and the gangs that sold them. People wanted serious firepower to fight a very real threat. Fear is an instinct and it is the basis of self-preservation. Guns are a response to the fear.

At the same time as Midwesterners wanted assault rifles, handguns came into demand. A handgun is a gun for close protection, usually an urban gun. It has a short barrel and, therefore, a very short range within which any shot is accurate. Its advantage, of course, is that a handgun can be carried on the person. People in the Midwest bought handguns as soon as they felt that the threat was a close one, walking down a street, in a parking garage, going home at night. Handguns have doubled in number in the last 25 years in America. That shows how immediate people's fears are.

The methamphetamine plague was the basic reason so many Midwesterners bought more guns in the 1990s, but there was a second impetus – the series of four violent events that took place in the 1990s and led to the mass shootings we are all too familiar with today. The first three of these events were politically right-wing and they were brutally spectacular, media-intense situations. The first was called "Ruby Ridge" and it took place in 1992. A family named the Weavers had been run out of a small town in northeastern Iowa. The Weavers were end-times evangelicals, hard-core fundamentalists. They were confrontational about their beliefs. Randy Weaver was fired from jobs for proselytizing. People thought they were organizing a cult. There was a series of complaints and police actions and finally, the Weavers left town. They moved to Ruby Ridge, Idaho.

You may remember hearing about all the right-wingers in the states of Montana and Idaho, the militias, survivalists and lone wolves. A lot of those extremists were not born in those two states. They were run out of small towns in the Midwest. Mr. Weaver was arrested in Idaho in a gun sting, and federal marshals tried to get him to inform on the Aryan Nations, once America's most prominent white supremacy advocates. Mr. Weaver refused. He was arrested on a trumped-up charge and given an incorrect date for his trial. When he didn't appear in court, because of the incorrect information, U.S. Marshalls were sent to arrest him. He refused to surrender. The conflict escalated into a twelve-day standoff during which there were hundreds of federal and state police surrounding the Weavers' tiny cabin on Ruby Ridge, and then a firefight erupted. In what is thought to be one of the most difficult sniper shots ever taken, an FBI sniper shot and killed Randy Weaver's wife, Vicki. Vicki had been the family's political leader and many people think it was Vicki who had been the target all along. Also killed were the Weavers' son and a U.S. Marshall. The media attention was intense and the critics of the government's actions were many. A Senate investigation uncovered the sheer amount of misinformation that had been given to Randy Weaver and to the agents working the case. Much of the blame for the violent action was placed squarely on the government agencies involved.

The Department of Justice then moved the federal team that was responsible for Ruby Ridge straight to the crisis in Waco, Texas, where they made all the wrong decisions once again. The Branch Davidian group was a fundamentalist Christian church led by David Koresh. They lived in a large communal compound outside the town of Waco. Koresh had been accused of statutory rape and polygamy and the compound was thought to be stockpiling illegal weapons. The Bureau of Alcohol, Tobacco and Firearms approached the compound with a search warrant and a gun battle ensued that resulted in 10 deaths. In response to the gunfight, the FBI laid siege to the compound and began a standoff that lasted 51 days. Finally, the FBI launched a tear gas attack and an immense fire started that ripped through the compound, quickly burning it to the ground. 76 Branch Davidians lost their lives. Americans watched on television as the buildings of the compound went up in flames. The conflagration was broadcast live. The date of the fire was April 19, 1993.

During the siege at Waco, Timothy McVeigh visited the site. He was already filled with anger at the situation in Ruby Ridge and visiting Waco increased his fury. On April 19, 1995, exactly two years after the fatal fire in Waco, McVeigh used a truck bomb to blow up the Murrah Building in Oklahoma City, Oklahoma. McVeigh killed 168 people and injured over 680 others. He was arrested, tried and, six years later, executed by lethal injection.

McVeigh not only committed the largest act of domestic terrorism in the United States, it was McVeigh who set the initial template for the mass shootings that were to follow. McVeigh understood the media message of a monstrous attack. He carefully picked the scene of the explosion so the media could get clear visuals of the devastation. After considering many potential sites, McVeigh chose the Murrah Building because the block across the street contained a parking lot which would allow cameras an unencumbered view of the bombed building. The building had a glass façade, which, when bombed, would become flying glass shards and create further injuries. It also contained offices of the Drug Enforcement Administration, the United States Secret Service, and the Bureau of Alcohol, Tobacco, and Firearms, all of which played into McVeigh's anti-government propaganda message. And finally, the Murrah Building housed a day care center. McVeigh wanted a high kill number because he knew that the higher the number of deaths, the greater the horror and therefore, the greater the publicity. And killing 19 children, as he did, brought furious anger, which meant even more attention. McVeigh stated later that he did not know a day care center was located in the building, but that was disputed by his friends.

Timothy McVeigh grew up in a small town in northwestern New York state. His family was classically blue-collar; his father worked in a factory that manufactured automobile radiators. Tim was brought up in gun culture. His grandfather taught him how to shoot when he was young and he became an extraordinary shot. He joined the U.S. Army, which he loved, and was sent to the Persian Gulf in Operation Desert Storm. On patrol, as the gunner in a Bradley Fighting Vehicle, McVeigh saw an Iraqi army machine gun nest a mile away. Ordered to shoot, he not only took out the Iraqi gunner, the explosive round he fired also killed the Iraqi shooter next to him. McVeigh was awarded a Bronze Star and selected to tryout to become a member of the Special Forces, which was something he had always wanted. McVeigh went directly from the fighting in Kuwait to Fort Riley, Kansas, where he had trained, to report in. Then he traveled to Fort Bragg, North Carolina, to test for the Army's elite fighting force, the Green Berets. He had just spent three exhausting months in combat in the desert and he was out of shape. The Army offered him a postponement so he could rest and prepare, but McVeigh thought that would be a sign of weakness. He began the Special Forces testing process and failed. That failure changed his life.

McVeigh left the Army and drifted through gun culture. He was angry and bitter. Special Forces had always been his goal and now, he had nothing. He took to the gun show circuit, became a survivalist and began to urge his friends to read anti-government propaganda, including *The Turner Diaries*, a novel written by William L. Pierce. The novel describes the actions of a character named Eric Turner, who protests the tightening of gun laws by blowing up the Washington, D.C. FBI headquarters with a truck bomb. It was easy for McVeigh to actualize the fictional attack. He was brilliant at weapons and explosives. McVeigh parked the truck containing the 5,000 pound bomb he had created from ammonium nitrate and nitromethane in front of the Murrah Building and destroyed it, as planned.

Suddenly, there was stunningly high-profile violence in mid-America. These three right-wing events, Ruby Ridge, Waco and the bombing of the Murrah Building in Oklahoma City, demonstrated the extraordinary amount of media attention a violent incident could capture. Television cameras and newsmen had covered the standoff at the Weavers' tiny cabin on a hill in Ruby Ridge for weeks. Millions of people watched the siege of the Branch Davidian compound and its apocalyptic fire. Scenes following the bombing in Oklahoma City broke viewers' hearts as police officers removed the broken bodies of dying children from the shattered building. And we watched it all.

The violence of those three events built from a shootout on a small Idaho hill to the hellfire of a dozen burning buildings in Waco to the massive devastation of a building hit by a 5000 pound bomb. While the first two incidents were the result of government standoffs, McVeigh's event was planned, staged even. His event was political. The bombing of the Murrah Building was the first major incident that was designed for the media.

And then, the ante was upped. The political message was dropped, the bomb was changed to a gun, and media was used as a platform to gain instant infamy. We moved into an era of what I call "media event mass shootings." A mass shooting is defined as a shooting in which three or more people are killed that occurs in a public place and is not domestic or criminal in nature. Mass shootings have enormous psychological impact because they are terrorism and terrorism works.

Having had a father who was thought to be insane enough to open fire, the one thing that has always struck me about murderers (and potential murderers) is their arrogance. These are men who are so psychopathically self-centered, they believe that the hurt the world has caused them is so deep and so profound they have the right to act out their anger by taking the lives of innocent people. It's a kind of psychopathic arrogance and the Columbine killers had that in spades.

On April 20, 1999, two students at Columbine High School in Littleton, Colorado, shot and killed 13 people before committing suicide. Eric Harris and Dylan Klebold had planned the attack for over a year. They were very specific about using Timothy McVeigh's action in Oklahoma City as a model. The two kept detailed journals in which they spoke of their intention to "outdo" the Oklahoma City bombing. They wanted a higher body count than McVeigh. Columbine High School had 2000 students and their plan, had it worked, would probably have killed at least half that number. Like McVeigh, the basis of their attack was intended to be explosives, in this case, a series of bombs. You can kill more people with bombs than with guns. The original attack date was set for April 19, 1999, the anniversary of both the Waco and Oklahoma City incidents, but the Columbine killers were forced to wait until April 20 to collect the ammunition they needed.

Unlike McVeigh, the Columbine killers did not plan to survive their attack; they thought they would either be killed by police gunfire or commit suicide. Also, unlike McVeigh, they purposely left an enormous amount of evidence. Their motivation was not political; they were obsessed with fame. Throughout the year before the action, they both kept journals and notebooks in which they methodically detailed their preparations. They listed the guns and ammunition they bought and the explosive devices they were building. They made drawings of the way the weapons, bombs and ammunition would be carried on their bodies. They detailed the timeline of their action. Harris built a private website with blogs that contained instructions for building bombs. The two killers made numerous videotapes and audiotapes in which they ranted about their lives and the people they hated. They wondered who would direct the film about them. Would it be Tarantino or Spielberg?

Harris and Klebold amassed an arsenal of guns and bombs. On the day of the massacre, Harris carried two guns, a pump-action shotgun and a carbine (short) rifle. Klebold used a TEC-9 semi-automatic handgun and a double-barreled shotgun. The barrels and butts of the shotguns were sawed off to make them easier to hide under the long black coats they wore. Harris used his two guns for a total of 121 shots, Klebold's total was 67 shots. That's a total of 188 shots and dozens of small bombs used in the attack. They had built 99 small explosive devices, some filled with shrapnel and homemade napalm, and they packed the small bombs in their backpacks.

The attack on Columbine High would proceed in three stages. The first stage would be a massive explosion in the school cafeteria, timed as the first lunch shift of 600 students filled the room. The main explosive devices, hidden in duffel bags, were two bombs created from 20-pound propane gas tanks wired to gasoline cans with a timer. These two bombs were potentially so powerful their explosion would create a fireball that would sweep through the school and destroy it. Hundreds would die. In the second stage, as the bombs exploded, the two killers would position themselves near the main school entrance and open fire on panicked students who were running from the flaming building. The third stage would be the detonation of more propane gas bombs that would be stashed in each of their cars, linked to gasoline cans and set to go off with timers. These bombs would kill police and emergency personnel responding to the scene and, the killers hoped, media. This final explosion would be televised live.

The cafeteria opened and the first lunch shift began at 11:00 and Klebold and Harris could not plant the two duffel bags containing the propane bombs until then. The bombs were wired to go off at 11:17, so the killers had 17 minutes to enter the cafeteria, plant the bombs, go back to their cars, arm themselves and get ready to shoot terrified survivors rushing from the building. They left the duffel bags in the sea of backpacks in the cafeteria and returned to their cars and waited. 11:17, 11:18, 11:19. No explosion. The propane bombs had failed. The heart of the attack was an apocalyptic explosion and it did not happen. Harris decided the only action that was possible now was to attack students using gunfire. They had not wanted an attack by gunfire but they had no choice. Harris grabbed his gear, ran to Dylan's car and the two of them rushed towards the school, opening fire. Harris hit two students eating in the grass. One died instantly, the second was hit and lost consciousness. The killers entered the school and ran through the hallways, throwing bombs and shooting at anyone they saw. The students stampeded to get out, faculty called 911 and ordered trapped students to hide, kids called their parents, a police officer assigned to the school fired on the killers. Columbine was chaos. Hundreds of students ran in mobs towards different exits. Everyone who was trapped in the building hid as best they could. Eric and Dylan were reportedly laughing the whole time. "This is awesome," one of the killers screamed. In the first five minutes, Harris and Klebold had killed two students and wounded ten.

It was 11:29 when the killers entered the library, the scene of the greatest carnage. Teachers had told the 52 students in the room to hide but hiding places were few. Most of the students were under tables. Harris yelled "Get up!" When no one did, he began shooting beneath tables and desks. It was in the library that Eric Harris realized his dreams of tyrannical cruelty. This was the moment all his hatred had prepared him for. He stalked the library, picking people off one by one and taunting them with remarks like "Peek-a-boo" and "Who's ready to die next?" He would choose someone, shoot and wound them, then deliver the death shot and move on to his next victim. Remember, in many instances, the killers knew their victims. With a gun pointed at him, a friend of Klebold's found the nerve to ask him what they were doing. Klebold responded, "Oh, just killing people." The seven minute rampage in the library took the lives of ten students and injured twelve more.

The two left the library at 11:36 and walked through the hallways, throwing bombs and shooting aimlessly. They had become bored. At one point, Klebold said, "Maybe we should start knifing people, that might be more fun." They wandered into the cafeteria, now almost empty, and took shots at the duffel bags in an attempt to make the bombs hidden inside explode. A small fire broke out that was rapidly extinguished by the sprinkler system. The cafeteria was a sodden mess and that was all. Their grand plan of conflagration was not to be. In a school videotape, the two looked depressed and defeated. It was as if they didn't know what to do next. A witness hiding in the cafeteria heard one of them say, "Today the world's going to come to an end. Today's the day we die." The two terrorists returned to the library and shot themselves. Their school rampage had killed 13 people and wounded 22.

From the minute the police officer on campus radioed in at 11:23 that there was a "female down," local police rushed to the school. Two officers who were nearby drove to the campus and found students who had been wounded by gunfire. As the officers were helping them, Harris fired in their direction and a gunfight broke out. Students were now rushing from the building to take cover behind the police car. They told the police that gunmen were shooting in the school and the officers called in "officer needs emergency assistance." In police talk, this means "get the hell over here," and area police started swarming towards the school. 911 calls were being made by students and teachers and frantic reports on police scanners were heard. The media moved like greased lightning.

It was at 11:32, when there were still only three police officers on the scene and Harris and Klebold were in the midst of massacring students in the library, that the first phone calls from reporters were answered in the Sheriff's Office. The reporters had heard something about a school shooting. Boulder, Colorado was 40 miles away and it was full of media crews digging for information on the Jon Benet Ramsay case. When they heard the first 911 calls on the scanners, they rushed to Columbine, ignoring police orders, driving straight onto the campus lawn. Hey, they had footage to get. Denver was even closer, a mere 12 miles away. Columbine was their turf. Local news channels immediately began full-time coverage of the shooting in progress, before they had any real information. The news spread like electronic wildfire and soon all of America was spellbound in horror, watching students running from the building as ambulances rushed the wounded to hospitals.

The cameras caught it all, terrified students running from the school, crying parents grasping their children, SWAT teams with long guns everywhere, shell-shocked students answering media questions, and the horrifying scene of a wounded student throwing himself out of the library window in desperation to leave the building. It was all broadcast live. It was as though we were there.

Of course, hundreds and hundreds of media people showed up. They arrived while the massacre was unfolding and stayed for weeks. It was a logistical nightmare for the authorities. They set up phone banks, a media communications center and tents for the reporters to live in. The day after the shooting, cellphones began to die. The sheer quantity of calls had eaten the power in the cellphone towers. Temporary towers were brought in and more phone banks were installed. The media had to have its juice.

And that was how Harris and Klebold got what they wanted. It was the media that gave it to them. The two killers wanted their nightmare of hatred to live on in the imaginations of people as full of hate as they were. And it has. Columbine replaced Oklahoma City as the terrorist template. Harris and Klebold had envisioned their destruction to be so large, to encompass so many aspects of an attack, it has inspired mass murderers everywhere. The number of successful and unsuccessful mass murderers who have stated that Columbine was their model is terrifying and it is due to the media, the media that sensationalized it in 1999 and the social media that has kept the story alive. Remember, Columbine happened in 1999, long before the Internet and social media were as powerful as they are today. When Harris and Klebold were documenting their actions, keeping journals, making videotapes, building websites, they thought they were leaving a story-telling trail. They thought they were letting the world know how they felt and why they did what they did. Little did they know that they were creating a cult, and that is what Columbine has become, it is a cult. Klebold and Harris left a large repository of documents and images and all of it is repeated endlessly on hundreds of fan sites dedicated to the online subculture of Columbine. For wannabe psychos, Klebold and Harris were the authors of a cultural script complete with gory details. Just do what they did, the fan sites seem to say, and you, too, will be glorious avengers.

There is a long list of examples of the Columbine effect. *Mother Jones*, the online news site, has developed a Columbine-copycat database. Its writers studied 74 attempts by potential shooters who said they had been inspired by Harris and Klebold. 53 of these attempts were stopped by police and 21 were carried out. In many of the plots, the would-be killers intended to attack on the anniversary of Columbine. They wanted a higher body count than Columbine. And most considered Klebold and Harris to be their idols. The Virginia Tech gunman, Seung-Hui Cho, called the Columbine killers "martyrs." One hopeful mass murderer decorated his gun with photos of Harris and Klebold. Copycats have carried the same guns and worn the same clothes. Dylan Klebold's mother receives letters from girls telling her how much they love her son. There are rock bands who write songs praising the Columbine killers. Columbine High School administrators speak of the problems they have with young guys who visit the school because they want to feel closer to the killers with whom they identify. They want to see the campus, check out the cafeteria, imagine which victim was sitting where in the library, take a souvenir. The potential killers look to Harris and Klebold not only for inspiration but for lessons. They study the operational details of the school shooting and argue about what went right and what went wrong. They plan their own crimes with the same obsessive detail Eric Harris used. Columbine has taught them that mass murder is not an impulse crime. Everything must be planned. Thanks to social media, the Columbine cult lives on.

After Columbine, so many of the mass murders had similarities. They took place in enclosed spaces, often schools, where the victims could be trapped. The spaces were gun-free zones, schools, churches, movie theaters, nightclubs, which the shooters had checked. The killers all used guns, not bombs, and the guns were usually semi-automatic rifles or semi-automatic handguns, which can kill large numbers of people in a short period of time. The perpetrators understood that the more gruesome the death they inflicted, the more publicity they would receive, so they went for children in school, African-Americans in church, dancers in a disco. Many shooters were aware of the sheer numbers of victims that mass shooters had killed previously and they tried to get a higher number in a grisly form of competition. Most of them intended to commit suicide at the event's end. The shooters were, for the most part, white males in their teens or twenties whose families were middle- or upper-middle class. They were often well-educated. And most of them were, or had been, on drugs, in a number of instances, psychotropic drugs.

There are almost no recent shooters who do not have extensive drug use in their pasts with the exception of those influenced by radical Islam. The first three violent situations in the 1990s were Ruby Ridge, Waco and Oklahoma City and they were caused by men with working class backgrounds. I find no evidence that Randy Weaver of Ruby Ridge or David Koresh of Waco used drugs. It is said that Timothy McVeigh of Oklahoma City had used amphetamines briefly but disliked drugs and quit using.

But beginning with Columbine, both the social class and the history of drug use by mass violence instigators changed radically. Mass murder was no longer the province of the drug-free working class. Now it was middle and upper-middle class males, many of whom had taken psychotropic (psychiatric) drugs. It was in the 1980s that psychiatry dropped the idea of talk therapy and began using drugs to treat conditions from depression and anxiety to schizophrenia and bipolar disorder. These drugs, psychotropic drugs, became common in the 1990s. They are drugs like Prozac, Valium and Zoloft, drugs that are advertised on television with warning phrases like "can increase your risk of suicide" and "violent side effects may including homicidal ideation."

The following is a list of mass murderers who have reportedly taken the listed psychotropic drugs. I have no way of making certain that these named drugs are correct but they were found on fairly responsible websites.

Eric Harris, Columbine High School, Littleton, Colorado, April 20, 1999, Zoloft and Luvox

Dylan Klebold, Columbine High School, Littleton, Colorado, April 20, 1999, reportedly Paxil and Zoloft; medical records have not been released

Seung-Hui Cho, Virginia Tech, Blacksburg, Virginia, April 16, 2007, Prozac

James Holmes, Century 16 Movie Theater, Aurora, Colorado, July 20, 2012, Zoloft, Clonazepam

Adam Lanza, Sandy Hook Elementary School, Newtown, Connecticut, December 14, 2012, had been prescribed Lexapro and Celexa; medical records have not been released but when the State of Connecticut was sued to have Lanza's medical records released to the public, the request was denied because "it would cause a lot of people to stop taking their medications"

Aaron Alexis, Washington Navy Yard, Washington, D.C., September 16, 2013, Trazodone

Dylann Storm Roof, Emanuel African Methodist Episcopal Church, Charleston, South Carolina, June 18, 2015, Suboxone, not prescribed, reportedly Xanax

Christopher Sean Harper-Mercer, Umpqua Community College, Roseburg, Oregon, October 1, 2015, reportedly Lithium; his mother, a nurse, had placed her son in a psychiatric hospital "when he did not take his medication"

And to add, it's an international problem:

Mohamed Lahouaiej-Bouhlel, killed 86 people by driving a truck down a boulevard in Nice, France, July 14, 2016, Haldol, Tranxene, Elavil

Andreas Lubitz, Germanwings Flight 9525 Co-pilot, killed 150 people by deliberately crashing his plane into the French Alps on March 24, 2015, Lorazepam

I want to add that Adolf Hitler was addicted to any number of drugs, amphetamines among them. In Iowa, amphetamines are called "Nazi dope" for a reason.

This is a very personal opinion, but I'm going to offer it. I think it's possible that, without their drugs, these men would not have been able to kill. Here's why. A large percentage of criminals who are caught have either cocaine or speed in their bloodstream. Those criminals take those drugs because the drugs give them the extra psychological push they need. Committing a crime is a very aggressive act and often, to get that aggression up and running, criminals need drugs. The mass shootings take something even more. The men who commit these shootings are not like you and me when we're having a bad day. These men inhabit a completely different psychological space. You and I can't imagine what that space looks like. Getting to the point where you're going to shoot someone, where you're going to open fire, is such an act of aggression that it requires a demonic energy. I think it's the drugs that give that energy to these men. Committing an atrocity, particularly a face-to-face mass murder, takes an inhuman amount of energy and a feral anger. It is even more difficult if the human targets are children. It's hard enough to get soldiers to open fire in a person-to-person situation in battle. To open fire on a group of helpless children is such an act of evil you and I could never do it. These killers know that they are harming more than the children. They are harming all of us.

I read a statement by a psychiatrist who was writing about the way we use words like "schizophrenic" and "bipolar" as adjectives. Those words have become so common we think we know what they mean. And then, the psychiatrist said, you meet a real one, a real schizophrenic or bipolar personality, one that's full-blown, and you stand back and go, "Oh, my God." It's stunning when you see a mental illness that's full-blown. It's overwhelming, it's unreal. What is mental illness? I dealt with this question the whole time I was dealing with my father. I have no idea how he would have been diagnosed. All I know is that he lived in a world where he got to make up the rules and they could change at a moment's notice. My father was an aggressive and hostile man. I thought he was like a cobra, an animal that watches you and moves and moves and waits until you show some sign of weakness and then strikes with all its force. Those strikes hurt. My father knew it. This was a man who had control over my life. His entire relationship to me was letting me know how much power he had over me. The rage my father had was what I call "annihilation rage." It was anger with intent to kill. It was terrifying.

CHAPTER 3
ON THE RUN

Remember, I wrote this book to explain my personal jour-
ney toward an understanding of my right-wing father and
his world. You will never hear a story like mine from anyone else.
Actually, there are many people in mid-America who have fathers
as deeply disturbed as mine, but their fathers tend to be men like
Ken McElroy of Skidmore, Missouri. McElroy was an infamous
local criminal whose life of crime was stopped in a classic case
of Midwestern vigilantism. McElroy raped, robbed, assaulted and
shot citizens of the town of Skidmore, and law enforcement did
nothing to stop him, apparently because they were so frightened
of him. In the summer of 1981, McElroy shot a man who lived.
McElroy threatened to finish the job. The townspeople held a
meeting. McElroy had a drink in the local tavern and got into his
pickup truck. People formed a crowd around him. Shots rang out.
McElroy was killed. No one knew whose bullet killed him. No one
saw anything. No one was charged with the crime. McElroy is a
perfect example of "white trash" run amok. He is exactly the type
of psychopath people try to force out of town before the shooting
starts.

Many people who have criminal psychopaths for fathers end up as drug addicts or alcoholics. Having a relative who commits serious criminal acts, particularly murder, has horrible psychological consequences for family members. That level of evil is so vile that many people close to the criminal simply can't assimilate it into their psyches and choose to blot it out with whatever substance is handy. I did not have to do that, and the reason is class.

Men like my father are almost always lower class, "white trash" if you prefer, in my father's case, Northern white trash. Dad was a doctor but he identified as lower class, which his father was. As they say, there ain't no fixing white trash. My father loved his lower class identity and refused to surrender it to his status as a doctor. It made him feel righteous and it gave him the excuse he wanted to feel like a victim. It allowed him to feel oppressed.

Children of white trash are never educated, particularly the female children. My mother died when I was fourteen and my father, true to his class identity, refused to give me money to go to college. He did not believe women should be educated. Lack of education meant women were financially dependent upon their husbands, and men like my father believed it was their duty to make sure their daughters were not capable of supporting themselves.

The money for my college came from my mother's family; they also got me away from my father after college when I moved to New York to live with my mother's sister. I had a real, old-fashioned class conflict in my own family and it saved my life. My mother's family had been upper class, robber barons from Minnesota who had lost much of their money in the depression but kept their liberal politics and their sense of class. They did not like my father at all.

I was born in Lake City, Minnesota, in February of 1942. World War II was beginning, and my father went into the Army. Mother and I went to live with her parents in Duluth. I spent most of the first four years of my life with my mother's family, happily ensconced in their comfortable, old-fashioned home. In the Army, my father didn't see any military action. He was stationed on bases in the South, in units whose goal was the protection of the Panama Canal. However, I have always believed that the Army knew how violent my father was and felt that if they sent him into battle, he would probably shoot his commanding officer. My father hated anyone he thought of as an authority figure and it was the kind of hate that came with a gun.

When my father was discharged from the Army, Mother and I moved with him back to his hometown, Lake City, and our lives went straight to hell. As soon as we moved in with him, we were on the run. We didn't have a house of our own, and one landlord after another fought with Dad and threw us out. I remember moving from place to place to place, and each place was cheaper, dirtier and meaner than the one before. The first house we moved into was a big square white house in the middle of town. One night at dinner, I didn't want to eat my peas. Dad turned toward me and screamed, right into my face, spitting at me in the process, "You eat your peas, young lady, I work hard to put food on this table, you eat every single thing on your plate," whereupon I began to cry. No one had ever screamed at me before. My grandparents didn't care what I ate. My mother told me to leave the dining room, she said something to Dad, and he never yelled at me in Mother's presence again. But whenever I was alone with him, he screamed. He could never just speak to me. His words were always filled with anger. This is why I do not accept the idea that psychopaths are out of control. My father knew exactly when he couldn't get away with his abusive behavior.

Shortly after that, Mother sent me to Duluth and when I returned, we had moved to Grandfather's cabin, where we lived for the summer until we moved into a house on the wrong side of town. I was in kindergarten now. After six months in this house, Dad had some kind of fight, I expect with the landlord, and we had to move again. This time, my mother knew Dad was in real mental trouble and she went to Duluth to ask her mother if she could leave my father and move back in to the Duluth house. Grandmother must have told her no. My mother was stuck in a marriage to a psychopath.

Now we moved to a motel out on Highway 61, then to an old farmhouse. It was in this farmhouse that I saw that my father realized he was mentally ill. He had a moment of clarity. Dad and I were playing cards one Sunday afternoon. Mother was in the kitchen. My father looked at me and quietly said, "Shug, we have to move again." He was crying. He knew there was something terribly wrong with him and he didn't know what it was. He could see that he was putting his wife and child through hell. He looked at me with pleading eyes, as if he were asking me to help him, to fix it. I was seven years old. It's a terrible problem to have a mentally ill parent. You want to love them so much but you have to protect yourself. If they see you as vulnerable, they can turn on you and attack. We did move again, to a summer cabin, and now we were as far out of town, as far out on Highway 61, as we could get. There was nowhere else to move. We were homeless and broke. Dad took a job as a salaried physician on an Army hospital base in Iowa.

When we finally left town and moved to Iowa, Dad became silent. For years, I only saw him at dinner. I had a kid brother by then. We never did anything as a family, no vacations, no picnics, no visits to cousins. It was as though my father were a balloon that had been deflated. All his fighting in Lake City had been a kind of an energy cell for him and now it was gone. He had lost. He was like a dog, walking off with his tail between his legs. That's exactly what vigilantes want. They don't want to physically harm the targets of their wrath, they want to humiliate them. Humiliation is much more painful.

My mother died seven years later, and I was left with my father. I knew I was in trouble. My mother had been my protection, and now my protection was gone. My father told me he would not give me money for college and he would not allow me to learn to drive. Then, my father addicted me to amphetamines, the drug he used. He told me I had to take the drug because I was getting fat, but I know the real reason he addicted me. A daughter will leave a hostile father, but a drug addict will never leave her supplier.

That drug was a nightmare. It grabs your brain and speeds you up so much you don't know who you are, and then you crash into a black amphetamine hole. I thought my father was trying to kill me. I was trapped and terrified and then, suddenly, I was saved. My mother's mother died and left me a small amount of money, which my father tried to take but lawyers stopped him. I dropped out of high school, got into college early, graduated and moved to New York to live with my mother's sister. I had a drug habit to beat and I needed help. I am the only person who ever ran away to New York to get off drugs.

My father was insanely angry. He ordered me back to Iowa and arranged a marriage for me. I declined. I did break my drug habit with the help of a psychiatrist, but I didn't know what had happened when I was young so I couldn't fix my broken self. I was so angry with my father I was feral. My anger ran my life. The only people who would put up with me were the anti-war movement kids at Columbia University, where I was a graduate student in political science, some gays friends in Greenwich Village who had also run away from small towns and a bunch of hippie musicians who kept feeding me weed to calm me down.

I not only couldn't talk about what my father was like, I couldn't think about it. All I could do was react with my anger. I'm lucky to be alive. I finally mentioned to my best friend from childhood that my father had refused to give me money for college. She became furious, and I knew I was on to something. I spoke about my father more often to my friends, and then, in 2007, I talked about him with my father's adopted sister, my adorable Aunt Mabel, who was living in Winterset, Iowa. Mabel was 99 years old and on her deathbed. She guessed that I didn't know everything about my father, and she was the last person alive who had been there to see what he had done. She knew that if she didn't tell me, I would never know.

Mabel and I had long phone conversations. She began speaking about my father with great hesitation. She probably had never talked about him before and she was afraid. I could hear the fear in her voice. My father had been dead for 30 years and his sister was still afraid of him. My aunt started by talking about his temper. She said he had had violent rages when he was a child and in order to stop him, my grandfather would kick him. My father would curl up in a little ball and duck his head, and my grandfather would kick him around the room like a soccer ball. Aunt Mabel said that both men had had this "rage that just exploded out of them" and, once it got started, nothing could stop it. She said it was "in the blood, it was something in the blood."

As he grew up, Mabel told me that my father fought with everyone and set up cycles of revenge. When he came back to Lake City after the Army, he was worse. Now he was threatening people with his gun, and people thought he was going to open fire, so they organized to run him out. It was Mabel who told me about the methods they used, about the boycott of his medical practice. My father was one of three doctors in a town of three thousand people, and if there's one person a town never runs out, it's its doctor. She also told me that my father was having a house built, and every time the house was framed out, men would go in with sledgehammers and knock it down. She was the one who told me that my father fought with the landlords, and that was why we had to move so often.

My father was incapable of understanding or modifying his own behavior. It was as if he had no objectivity. Everything came from far inside himself; everything was subjective and emotional. He couldn't bond with people and that meant that he lived in psychological isolation. His anxiety and anger would build up and with no relationships he could use to siphon them off, he lived in misery until he eventually exploded. Mabel couldn't understand how my father could be both so smart and so dumb. She said he had everything to live for, but his behavior was so self-destructive. My father was trapped inside his own fears.

My aunt also talked about the world my father grew up in. He had been born in 1912 in "old Minnesota," as Aunt Mabel called it. She meant German-America, the German Belt. In those days, the Germans ran the Midwest. People don't talk about it, but as Germany built toward Nazism in the 1920s and 1930s, there was a parallel movement in America, a very powerful pro-German, anti-Semitic movement. It was called an isolationist movement, but most of the anti-war groups were organized by German-Americans. That movement was so powerful it kept the United States out of World War II for 27 months after Hitler invaded Poland, 27 months that allowed Hitler to conquer most of Europe. The German-American senators from the Midwest worked with Southern senators to prevent FDR from giving aid to England. That pro-Nazi movement was only stopped because the Japanese bombed Pearl Harbor. If Pearl Harbor hadn't been bombed, America probably would not have entered the war.

When the war was over, Mabel said my father didn't change. He still clung to the old right-wing ideology, the Aryan sense of superiority and the theory of patriarchy, the ideology that said that the father had absolute power, that the wife and the children were servants and were to be treated as such.

What my Aunt Mabel told me was a shock to my system, a real physical shock. At one point, my body lost all its warmth. My blood had run cold. I couldn't believe I had had a father like that. I was insane with anger. My mind couldn't accept it all at once. The awareness came in shock waves. I would remember something he had said and I would get hit by the recognition of what it really meant, and then I would have to shut down for a while, and then another memory would come back and hit me and I would try to assimilate that. Those memories are still coming back to me. My father was deeply, unfathomably ill, twisted with hate. He destroyed my mother and he almost got me. And do you know why my mother and I allowed that to happen to us? Because Mother and I were liberals. We did not believe in evil.

After Aunt Mabel told me the truth about my father, so many things made sense to me. The trauma of being run out of town had had a cause, the anger people felt toward us had had a reason, my terrible relationship with my father made complete sense. But as I thought it over, and I thought it over often, there was one thing I could not figure out. How did Lake City know how to run us out of town? The citizens of Lake City, who must have considered my father an imminent danger to throw out a doctor, did an excellent job of single-instance vigilantism. Granted, it had taken them three years to force the man to leave. But keeping up that kind of pressure for three entire years took determination and skill. And it took one more thing. It took knowledge. You don't just decide to force a man out of town. You have to know how to organize. You have to keep the pressure up for as long as it takes. How could they have known all this? Was it intuitive? Or was there a history of vigilantism in the area of which I was unaware? I Googled "vigilantism in Minnesota." I was stunned by what I found.

CHAPTER 4

ANTI-GERMAN VIGILANTISM IN 20TH CENTURY AMERICA

Minnesota, indeed, the entire Midwest, had produced a huge and violent vigilante movement in the 20th Century. I was born and raised in the Midwest and I had never heard about it. That vigilante movement was against German-Americans during World War I. The non-German Midwesterners had beaten the schnitzel out of the Krauts.

Here is how it worked. When the Germans migrated to America in the 1840s and 1850s, they didn't plan to immigrate and assimilate, they planned to colonize. They wanted to do to mid-America what the English had done to the colonies. As England had called the colonies "New England," the Germans called the Midwest "New Germany." They tried to buy the states of Texas and California. When that didn't work, they formed settlement societies in Germany and shipped over thousands of Germans at once. They took over the Midwest, from Ohio to the Rockies. Their superb organizing skills meant that, although they were per-haps one-quarter of the population, the Germans ran everything.

They ran the banks, the school systems, the farms, the newspapers, they ran it all and it was all in the German language. Let me repeat that. It was all IN THE GERMAN LANGUAGE. The means by which they intended to take over America was to change the language used from English to German. The bank records were in German, the newspapers were in German, THE TEACHERS TAUGHT SCHOOL IN THE GERMAN LANGUAGE. There were huge swaths of land in mid-America in which the English language was never heard.

The trouble started in 1917, upon the declaration of World War I. German-Americans went into active resistance, sending money to Germany, sending sons to fight on the German side and mounting an aggressive pro-German propaganda campaign in America. And then, Midwestern boys were called to sign-up for military duty. They showed up to register and they did not speak English. Mind you, they were third or fourth generation by now. America did not understand until that moment, until they saw the number of Midwestern sons who spoke only German, how much power the German-Americans had in the United States. Non-German Midwesterners were furious. The farmers took action. When a preacher gave a sermon in the German language, they burned his church down. When a schoolmaster taught classes in German, his school was torched. Many Germans were shot to death or lynched, many more were run out of town. People considered subversive were dragged out of bed in the middle of the night and brought to the town square where they were forced to pledge allegiance to the flag. But there was one big demand the public made: make it illegal to speak German. Laws against the use of the German language were passed in 26 states. That's 26 states that were so furious with German-American power, they passed laws intended to banish their language. In Iowa, the governor issued the "Babel Proclamation," which outlawed any language other than English.

In South Dakota, where the population was almost entirely German, the police listened to every telephone conversation and arrested anyone who spoke a single word in the German language.

But it was in Minnesota that people got serious. Minnesota was different from the rest of the Midwest in that it was industrialized and quite wealthy. The state had been the home of the lumber industry, it was now the home of the flour industry, and it had the highest quality iron ore in the country. Iron being the basis of steel, Minnesotans rose to great wealth based on the industrialization the country experienced after the Civil War. It was steel and its factories, its railroad rails, its machines, that catapulted men like Rockefeller, Carnegie, Vanderbilt and Morgan to power. Minnesota welcomed the Eastern industrialists with their fine educations and sophisticated tastes. Said industrialists were not happy with the German-Americans refusing to participate in their capitalist system. These robber barons were the "1 percent" of their day and that 1 percent held back nothing. They instituted a form of vigilantism I call "parallel government vigilantism." It was temporary full-on fascism. The governing body to this anti-German-American movement was run by a group called the "Minnesota Commission of Public Safety" ("MCPS"). Its purpose was to shut German-America down. It did.

The MCPS was a parallel government entity with its own courts, judges and police. It had dictatorial powers. It seized the private property of German-Americans, closed down hundreds of German-language newspapers and forced schools to stop teaching in German. Its police-state powers were extraordinary. It created its own militia, set up a court system to subpoena individuals suspected of subversive behavior and held hearings on groups that were accused of sedition. It was judge, jury and executioner. "One Country, One Flag, One People and One Speech" became the order of the day.

German-Americans gave up. They no longer called the Midwest "New Germany." It had taken massive vigilantism to force assimilation on German-America. The vigilantes did it in two years. That's how violent it was.

So now, I'm thinking, OK, where did Minnesota get this idea? And my serious study of gun culture and American vigilantism began.

CHAPTER 5
THE ROLE OF THE GUN

Historians tell us that the American Revolution was won because the citizens owned their own firearms. Colonists organized themselves into militias to fight the well-armed British troops, and those militias were so effective that, after the Revolutionary War, gun ownership was legally mandated. The argument is that the victory against the British troops was won by collective armed action and that is why the Second Amendment means so much to so many. The phrase "the right of the people to keep and bear Arms, shall not be infringed," means that the people have the right of armed revolt against a government that fails to represent them. The concept of popular sovereignty may be the strongest idea that grew in the new America. The will of the people was paramount and the right to own a gun ensured that.

The guns traveled with the settlers as settlement America was built. The truth is that the fruited plains were a land without laws. Guns were a necessary part of settlement survival. Settlers used guns for three reasons: One, to shoot dinner. Without guns, they couldn't feed their families. Two, for protection for their families from Indian raids and outlaws, and to keep wild animals from their stock. Three, to keep horse thieves from stealing their horses. The gun was a basic instrument of survival in a land without laws.

America was settled by dirt-poor people who went through absolute hell to get here. European peasants had just crawled out of serfdom. They had neither land nor jobs in Europe and many were starving. America had 2 billion acres of land, much of it free. Free land, the dream of every peasant in Europe. Those former serfs came by the millions, a great swarm of people desperate for land. They took huge risks. They got on tiny, rotting wooden ships that often sank in violent storms. The trip across the Atlantic could take between 12 and 20 weeks. The immigrants were packed in the belly of the ship like sardines. Starvation, cholera and the plague raged among the passengers with so many deaths that one out of every seven died along the way. They landed on the East Coast with no money and the trek across America began. To get to their plot of promised Midwestern land, sometimes immigrants took a railroad trip on a cattle car, sometimes they bought an ox and a little wooden wagon to haul their meager belongings and they walked the whole way. Their wagons were often so primitive, the wheels were logs. The trip to Minnesota could take months. There were no roads, only Indian trails, and those were rocky, narrow paths that had barely been cleared of trees, never of their stumps. There were no bridges; the settlers forded their way across rivers, often losing all the family's goods or even their lives. In rain or snow, the going was an endurance test. If the ox cart was big enough, the whole family slept in it. Otherwise, the family slept under the open sky.

When they got to Minnesota, the settlers lived in what they called "Minnesota mansions." These were gopher holes, a large hole dug straight into the ground or into the side of a hill, if they were lucky enough to have a hill. A thick rug served as their door. They lived in these windowless dirt caves for years. One step up in home design was what were called "soddies," sod huts which were built by cutting topsoil into long strips and laying them like bricks into round-roofed soil igloos. When it rained heavily, soddies had a nasty tendency to become mud.

And when they had settled, dug their gopher holes or built their soddies, they had to get to work planting and harvesting the wheat that would allow them to survive. These men and women lived lives of extreme hardship and deprivation. Farm work was exhausting, clearing the land, plowing, sowing and reaping. When the crops were finally harvested, they had to take them to market, a round-trip which could take a month. They suffered plagues of Biblical proportions. Grasshoppers came in swarms so thick they blotted out the sun and ate all the crops. Fire, driven by the wind at lightning speed, swept across the prairie grass in a sea of flame and destroyed everything in its path. Winters were vicious, with violent blizzards that caused livestock to freeze to death or be smothered by snow. Families were trapped in homes with 40-degree-below-zero cold and drifts that covered their houses, if they had houses. All contact with the outside world was closed, and many starved to death. Women, particularly German women, were in a constant state of childbearing, with only the husband to help during birth. There were no doctors, and midwives were miles and miles away. The rate of death in childbirth was high.

And if they survived the locust plagues and the winter blizzards and the diphtheria epidemics, if they survived Indian attacks, if women survived giving birth every year with only their husband to help, in a few years their wheat crop brought in money and they could build a wooden house with one room and a dirt floor and a tree bark roof. These houses measured several hundred square feet and often housed a dozen people. That truly was a mansion to them.

Those settlers came here desperate for land and they took it any way they could. Nothing stopped them. They led lives of horrible hardship and they would do anything to protect what they owned. Vigilantism and its violence came easily.

CHAPTER 6

VIGILANTISM BEGINS: ANTI-HORSE THEFT VIGILANTISM

In the settlement days, there wasn't any money for sheriffs or jails. All of America was, at one point, a frontier, and although property was quickly claimed and developed, the institutions that protected property were not. The farms and small settlement towns came first. The sheriffs, jails and courts came later. In most parts of the country, there simply was no law. The distance between settlement towns could be hundreds of miles. It was only the most established towns that had a sheriff. Their property being crucial to a frontier people's existence, when there was a community crime problem, people got together for protection. Vigilantism was born. Vigilantism was part and parcel of gun culture in America, present at its birth. It was the basis of law and order in our settlement days. America is the only nation that has had an extensive system of vigilantism. There is no state in the Union that was without vigilantes. Vigilantism, as the basis of early law and order, is part of the reason America has such a powerful gun culture. Gun culture was formed by the community need for self-preservation. It was an early definition of community in America.

The single crime that was the basis of the first vigilantism in America was horse theft. It was a crime that existed in every settlement in every state. In early America, horses were the center of the farm economy. It was the horse that was used to plow the fields and take the crops to town. All travel was by horse. Horses moved supplies and brought the mail. The loss of a horse often meant the loss of the family farm. Horses were so expensive that a farmer who lost his horse could seldom afford another.

Horse theft was common. It was easy to steal a horse: just find a moment when it wasn't watched, when it was tied up in town or grazing out in a pasture, and ride off on it. Horses were carefully guarded. People who needed to do business in town left their horse in a livery stable. A town without a stable often had a local drunk who would keep an eye out, for a small fee. If someone was spotted riding an animal that people thought didn't belong to them, the rider would be stopped and questioned. Everyone was on a constant watch for horse thieves. These thieves were particularly clever. They would follow a doctor on his way to visit a patient and, when the doctor tied the horse up and went into the home, they took the horse. A farmer bringing his crops to market would be ambushed by two or three thieves and his horse taken. If he were jumped in a remote area, he would be without a way to return to his family. It could be a death sentence.

Horse thieves operated in gangs; it was easier to move a horse out of a territory that way and, once out of the territory, it could be safely sold. Catching the gang required a group of men. They often had to pursue the criminals over a great distance, and that necessitated a group that could trade off pursuit duties. If the gang was caught, the confrontation would require multiple men to make the arrest or mete out justice. And the justice could be harsh. Many a horse thief ended up on the wrong end of a noose. Harsh punishments were believed to dissuade those with criminal inclinations, and those punishments, whippings, shootings, hangings, were always public. They sent a strong message.

Vigilantism in the settlements functioned almost entirely to control the theft of horses, but there existed a second kind of vigilantism, the "parallel government" type. The first notable instance of this second type of vigilantism occurred in the backcountry of the Carolinas. It was basically the seizure of state power by wealthy property owners who wanted to control property crimes that local law enforcement refused to deal with. These vigilantes called themselves "regulators." They hired small armies, arrested criminals, set themselves up as judge and jury, handed down sentences and threw men in jail. As soon as their problems were taken care of, the regulators disbanded. This early institution of regulators grew up to be the Minnesota Commission on Public Safety by way of the San Francisco Committee of Vigilance. Since the very beginning of American history, property protection was an aggressive industry.

West of the Alleghenies, it was a dogfight.

The great American West, from the Appalachian chain to the California shore, was one huge opportunity to an outlaw gang. Between the mighty Mississippi and the Pacific Ocean, vigilantism ruled for 40 years. That vigilantism was due to three things: the Gold Rush, the open range and the chaos caused by the Civil War.

CHAPTER 7

VIGILANTISM HITS THE BIG TIME IN SAN FRANCISCO

The mother of all vigilante groups was organized in, of all places, beautiful San Francisco. It was a virtual takeover of a corrupt city government by businessmen trying to cope with the crime resulting from the California Gold Rush. The San Francisco Committee of Vigilance was a kind of temporary fascism and it was entirely public, no secrecy, no apologies, no explanations, just a takeover that cleaned the town up and then disbanded. In order to understand the audacity of this vigilantism, you have to take a good look at the conditions created by the discovery of gold in California.

The story is simple. On January 24, 1848, a contractor blasted river rock to form a channel for a mill on the American River outside of Sacramento. Something glittered in the newly loosened gravel. It tested as gold and its discovery was reported in a San Francisco newspaper, but no one believed the report until the newspaper publisher rushed to open a store selling prospecting supplies, after which he ran through San Francisco's streets holding up a small bottle of gold yelling, predictably enough, "Gold,

gold!" The rush was on. The trick was that California was still legally a part of Mexico. The Mexican-American War ended on February 2, 1848, and California became a U.S. possession, not a territory or a state, a possession. As a possession, there were no courts, no legislature to pass laws and no laws regarding the use of the public land that held the gold. In gold-mining territory, there were no laws about property.

The other trick was that this was the type of gold that was called "placer gold." It was found in the form of small nuggets or dust in the rocky beds of streams. A person could collect it by panning; the tools needed were pans, picks and shovels, which anyone could afford. No property laws and cheaply mined gold plus national newspaper accounts of the discovery was a recipe for chaos. And the sheer quantity of gold in the California earth was staggering. Huge fortunes were made in the early days of the gold rush. The take from the strikes is estimated to have been tens of billions of dollars in today's currency.

People stormed the countryside. Every river, creek and stream was panned. Thousands of mining camps sprung up. Since there was no law regarding ownership of property, the miners used the old Mexican method of staking claims, which meant that the first person on a site owned it as long as he was working it. Claim jumping was common, as was sheer theft, and miners' courts settled small disputes. There were no jails in the camps and no law enforcement. As the stakes rose, the miners' courts turned violent, and soon there were hundreds of vigilante groups operating in California, solving problems by throwing men out of the camps, flogging or even hanging them.

When the gold was first discovered, San Francisco became a ghost town as its citizens abandoned everything to pan for the precious metal. Soldiers left their posts, businesses were closed, homes were shuttered, fields lay unharvested, newspapers shut down as there were no readers. Soon there were 500 ships rotting in San

Francisco Bay as their seamen deserted them for the gold fields. It was a stampede. These early claims could bring in $1,000 a day.

But then people began arriving via arduous overland routes and by ship from the American East Coast and the Pacific Rim nations, and the population decline was reversed. San Francisco, which had held about 800 people in 1848, grew to 5,000 by the next year. In 1849, an estimated 90,000 people arrived in California, and now they were coming from everywhere. Gold fever hit big and it hit hard. San Francisco became a boomtown.

But the immigrants brought problems. England had shipped many of its convicted criminals to prisons in Australia. These men, called "Sydney Ducks," made their way to San Francisco and formed Sydney Town, a small area on the outskirts of the little city. Sydney Town became a criminal underworld, a haven, a place the police did not enter. From Sydney Town, the Sydney Ducks made their forays into the city proper, where they did what they were good at—committing crime. They stole gold from miners, took men for their money in gambling dens, started fights in saloons. Murder became a frequent occurrence, adding up quickly to a count in the hundreds within a few months. The Sydney Ducks set fires that devastated neighborhoods, making the area easy to plunder. The Barbary Coast was born and with it, the San Francisco Committee of Vigilance. The Committee declared itself in operation on June 9, 1851, and, on June 10, 1851, hung one John Jenkins, from Sydney. That was just the beginning.

San Francisco's Committee of Vigilance was not your standard vigilante group. It was not a group of small-town citizens determined to put an end to property-threatening behavior at the point of a gun. This was a group of several hundred of San Francisco's property-owning elite, the wealthiest men in town. They seized power in armed opposition to the City's elected and appointed legislature, judiciary and police. They wrote a mission statement that documented their purpose and defined their goals. They published their names and announced their meetings. They formed a militia. They set up a parallel government that conducted trials, carried out executions by public hanging, forced politicians out of office, drove criminals out of town, deported undesirable foreigners and, generally, dealt quickly and efficiently with the enormous amount of crime that washed over San Francisco during the Gold Rush. Then, mission accomplished, they disbanded. They returned in 1856 to repeat their activities and disbanded again. A new model of vigilantism was born.

There were those who felt a dangerous precedent had been set. This was fascism in a port town. The truth is that very little is actually known about the workings of the San Francisco Committee of Vigilance, as most of the published material on the Committee was written by the Committee itself or by its supporters. It was a unique combination of factors that allowed this temporary takeover. California was a possession of the United States. The governmental structure, the court system, the legislature and law enforcement were a hodgepodge of common American practice and holdover systems from the Mexican days. Vigilantism was common in the gold fields. Everyone had guns. Enormous, unimaginable wealth had been created in a very short period of time, and a large criminal underworld went after that money. A vigilante group seized power, functioned as judge and jury and then left the power behind when the job was finished. The San Francisco Committee of Vigilance left two lasting legacies: it cleaned up San Francisco and it gave vigilantism a good name.

CHAPTER 8
VIGILANTISM GETS NASTY IN MONTANA

Another gold rush occurred in Montana with radically different results. Montana pretty much wins the title of most horrific vigilante mob action short of the Ku Klux Klan. Montana's gold rush happened in the early 1860s, a decade after the strike in California. The West was now full of prospectors searching for the next lode of gold, and they found it in Montana. That gold brought the bloodiest reign of vigilante violence the West had ever seen. Montana was part of the Idaho territory, and the territorial courts were unknown in the remote mining fields, which, as in California, used miners' courts to settle disputes. That situation, the lack of legal code, courts and law enforcement and the sheer quantity of criminals the gold attracted, led to murderous lawlessness and the inevitable formation of vigilante gangs who often simply killed anyone accused of jumping claims, robbing stagecoaches or rustling horses. They strung crooks up and then strung up a couple more people for good measure. They even lynched a sheriff they didn't like. But the sheriff, who was a noted gunfighter, was said to have been the head of a murderous gang, a gang that counted their victims in the hundreds. You couldn't tell the good guys from the bad guys, probably because they were often the same people.

When there were trials, they were held outside in the public square, and the often large audience was allowed to vote on whether the accused was guilty or innocent. The popular outlaws went free to kill again. This was not the San Francisco Committee of Vigilance. This was not a situation in a city in which a group of men set up a public structure parallel to the government in order to control crime. This was lynch mob vigilantism. Montana in its gold rush days was the perfect example of vigilantism run amok.

The round-them-up-and-kill-them attitude continued through the 1870s and 1880s, when Montana's ranches experienced significant cattle and horse thievery. The area the ranches covered was enormous and impossible to patrol, and organized, armed gangs were successfully stealing thousands of cattle a year. A rancher named Granville Stuart decided that aggressive action was necessary and formed a vigilantism group of fourteen men plus himself, known forever as "Stuart's Stranglers." The vigilante group found two rustlers, a corral full of stolen, branded horses and a barn full of fresh cowhides, ready to be brought to market for sale. The men lynched the rustlers, searched for more of the same, found two more and strung them up. Their success prompted them to raid an outlaw hideout, causing the deaths of an entire gang, and these attacks, having turned into a war of extermination, continued throughout the long, bloody summer of 1884. No one knows how many victims decorated trees courtesy of the vigilantes. Newspaper reports suggested the numbers were in the hundreds; others think it was merely several dozen unfortunate souls. The number didn't matter. Stuart's Stranglers became legend.

Those were the two extremes of Western vigilantism, the San Francisco Committee of Vigilance and Stuart's Stranglers. The two situations had a number of things in common: lack of law enforcement and legal code, immense, rapidly gained wealth and a plethora of desperados. But they had something else in common that is very important to understand about property protection vigilantism. The San Francisco Committee of Vigilance and Stuart's Stranglers were both groups made up of the wealthiest citizens in their respective societies. Most vigilante groups were not, as is commonly assumed, composed of individuals from the lower income classes, white trash bent on revenge. They were men of property, the community elite, people who were essentially conservative and wanted to preserve a society in which they governed and prospered. They saw crime not only as a threat to their personal wealth but as a larger threat to the very foundation of a stable, efficiently functioning community. The property-holding elite became the law when law enforcement was absent or incompetent. The wealthy intended to preserve the source of their wealth and they had the power to do so. The roster of former members of vigilante organizations and supporters of same includes a long list of governors and senators and two presidents, Andrew Jackson, of course, and Teddy Roosevelt. Roosevelt was refused membership in, of all groups, the Montana Vigilantes of 1884, Stuart's Stranglers.

CHAPTER 9
VIGILANTISM ON THE OPEN RANGE

The gold strikes in the West were a magnet for criminals. A second irresistible target was the open range, home of the cowboy. The open range was comprised of millions of acres of public-domain grazing land stretching from the Mississippi River to the Rocky Mountains. Herds of cattle were driven from their Texas ranches to the open range to feed and fatten up before the roundup that shipped them to market. The cattle were left to graze, limited only by rivers, mountains and tough terrain, and they could roam over thousands of miles. It made cattle rustling easy and very, very lucrative. Most of the rustlers were cowboys themselves and they knew the herds and the lay of the land. They could move in on an untended herd, drive it to a distant area or unpatrolled Indian territory, change the brand and sell the livestock at market.

The ranchers hired gunmen to protect their livestock, and these gunfighters, having been hired to serve as protection, often had a semi-legal status in working with lawmen. The hired guns did, of course, dispatch the bad guys when necessary, but they were a new kind of vigilante, one that operated with the law, not in place of it. This hired-gun vigilantism evolved into large-scale institutional private police enforcement such as the famed Pinkerton Detective Agency, which, at one point, employed more men than the U.S. Army. Vigilantism in the West was changing.

Vigilantism changed even further when it came to horse rustling. Horse theft was such a serious crime that an entire vigilante movement was born on the open range to stop the practice. These vigilantes and their actions were, however, within the scope of the law. They were called, appropriately enough, the "Anti-Horse Thief Association" (the "AHTA"). The AHTA was considered a vigilante group as it had no legal authority, but it worked with law enforcement and through the courts. When a horse was stolen, it was reported to the AHTA, which used the telegraph to spread the description of the animal and the thief to fellow members and to the law. A group of members would give chase and, with many people on the lookout, could often track the thief down. He was trailed until he was caught, turned over to the authorities and prosecuted. This network organization worked so well that it spread throughout the Midwest and had 30,000 members. The crime that had started America's system of vigilantism, the theft of horses, was finally under control and vigilantism gave way to law enforcement. It was about time.

CHAPTER 10

VIGILANTISM GOES EXTREME: THE KU KLUX KLAN

I t was the Civil War that brought America its worst example of vigilantism. America's Civil War and the chaos that followed led to the creation of the group most people think of when they think of vigilantes, the Ku Klux Klan (the "KKK"). The Klan was an extreme form of vigilantism, a militarily structured death squad. The difference between vigilantism and death squads is that vigilantism tends to be local, non-political and civilian. Death squads are large-scale terrorist campaigns associated with a political or governmental organization that uses extreme brutality and murder as method. The Klan was a killing machine. Nevertheless, the Klan was officially civilian, local and non-governmental, so it qualifies as part of any discussion of vigilantism.

The power of the KKK after the Civil War was extraordinary. The Klan was called the "Invisible Empire of the South." The North had won the War and had destroyed the South. The Klan stepped into the void.

The cotton gin had revolutionized the South. It was invented in 1793 and it was not a cotton engine, it was a cash machine. It caused the wealth of the South to explode. In 1860, the South produced 1000 times the number of bales of cotton it had produced in 1790. The newly rich South intended to keep the basis of its wealth, the slave system, and the North intended to end it. It was a ferocious fight. The South went from tremendous wealth to dire poverty in four years, the years of the Civil War, 1861 to 1865.

The true tale of the creation of the Klan is told by the method the North used during the Civil War to crush the system of slavery forever. Northern leaders, the heads of the Union Army as well as President Abraham Lincoln, believed that slavery was so much a part of the South that the only way to change the South was to destroy it. And that is what the Union Army did. It adopted a type of warfare called "total war." This meant that the economic base of the entire South, civilian as well as military, had to be smashed. To do that, the Union Army blockaded Southern ports, seized control of river traffic and damaged railroad tracks until they were beyond repair. Bridges, canals and roads lay in ruin. The Northern forces burned towns, demolished buildings and homes and ravaged farms, seizing or killing livestock and burning all the crops they couldn't use. Cotton gins and mills were razed. The South was the enemy, and anything that was useful to the enemy was destroyed. The South lay in ruins. There was nothing left, no factories, no farms, no jobs, no hope. It was fertile territory for the Klan.

The Klan was determined that the North would not rule the South. Most Klan leaders had been members of the Confederate Army and their intention was clear: restore white supremacy, destroy the Republican Party, drive Republicans out of the South, reverse the legal changes Reconstruction mandated, and prevent blacks from voting, owning land or building businesses. The first KKK organization (there were three) was in existence from the winter of 1865–66 to 1871, when Congress passed the 1871 Civil Rights Act (the "Ku Klux Klan Act"). The 1871 Act dismantled the Klan, which by then had become so outrageous in its anti-Republican and anti-black violence that many in the South had denounced it in fear of repercussions.

The Klan was born in the winter of 1865–66. The first presidential election after the Civil War was in November of 1868. Andrew Johnson had assumed the Presidency after President Lincoln was assassinated. Johnson had been a Democratic Senator from Tennessee who did not leave his seat when his state seceded, so Lincoln had chosen him as his Vice President in a show of unity. Johnson proved to be seriously unpopular and was impeached by the House. The Klan, fearing that the North would take the 1868 election with a Republican, knew they had a brief two-year period in which they would be free to destroy their enemy, Southern Republicans and newly-freed blacks who would vote.

They went to work and the violence they used was extreme. They terrorized Republican supporters and drove them out of towns. They murdered Republican Party leaders. The Klan was so successful in their brutality against the Republican Party that in many counties, there were no Republican votes cast at all. As for the blacks who were finally able to vote, the Klan assaulted them, dragged them from their homes at night, whipped them, lynched them, shot them and left their bodies by the road or hanging from trees for all to see. It was a slaughter. Hundreds of white people and thousands and thousands of blacks were killed. The Southern Democrats won. Reconstruction was reversed. Republicans were run out of the South. White supremacy was restored. The Democratic Party and Jim Crow ruled the South for 100 years. The Ku Klux Klan is a terrifying testament to the power of vigilantism and its violence.

CHAPTER 11

GUNS AND TEXAS

And finally, a brief word about Texas. You can't talk about vigilantism in America without talking about Texas. Early in its history, Texas seemed to hit some kind of critical mass of conflict that dissolved the entire society into a cranky bunch of gunfighters. Got a problem? Lock and load. Texas was practically its own model of vigilantism. Texas saw more, many more, vigilante movements than Montana. In Montana, vigilante movements were about property and property protection. Much of Texan vigilantism was a different sort of dogfight. Its vast land area contained many competing groups: Europeans, Mexicans, Native Americans and, later, freed African slaves. Texan vigilantism was often one group fighting another. And Texas was home to some of the most extraordinarily murderous family feuds in all of human history. Texas seemed to be a society that embodied the ethic of the Old West, that never quite got past its frontier days, and that turned to larger caliber ammunition to solve all its problems from the macro-political wars all the way down to the micro-political feuds. Texas was a society at war with itself. I think the reason for this determined belligerence goes back to its birth. Texas was defined by three main wars, the wars it fought to be free from Mexico, the wars fought with and by its Native American population and the vigilante wars resulting from the deluge of sheer lawlessness that engulfed the state when the criminal remnants of the beaten South went west after the Civil War.

From the very start, Texas was born in blood. It fought the Texas War of Independence to free itself from Mexico in 1836 because Mexico didn't want slavery and Texas had all that rich cotton-farming land that welcomed the plantation system, the slave economy of the Deep South. It fought Mexico again in the Mexican-American War of 1846–1848, when Mexico decided it wanted Texas back. But the big fight, the fight that I believe defined Texas as a state that felt it needed its guns, was the Indian War. Every state in America had Indian wars, that's how the American land mass was settled—run off the Native Americans and farm the land. The Native Americans, of course, did not want to go, and some nasty fights ensued, but none were as nasty, I think, as the Indian War in Texas. That war was due to a single Indian nation, the Comanches.

The Comanches were a uniquely violent tribe. They built an empire of 250,000 square miles called "Comancheria," which comprised land that is now central and west Texas, eastern New Mexico, Oklahoma and Kansas. Comancheria was the base from which the tribe made brutal raids into Mexico and then throughout Texas as it was settled. Those raids got the Comanches the horses and cattle they sold and the women and children they used as slaves. Often they ransomed the women and children, who were bought back by their families in horribly abused condition, the women having been raped and tortured. These raids took place from the early 1700s in Mexico into the 1870s in Texas. Comanche raids into Mexico were so successful and so frequent that northern Mexico was depopulated, looted, burned and destroyed, its people kidnapped or killed. Some of the Mexican raids were conducted by Comanche armies with thousands of warriors. Tens of thousands of Mexican men were killed. The estimate of the number of women and children kidnapped by the Comanches is 20,000.

The Comanches, with the wealth from their terrorist activities, became the dominant tribe in the Southwest. When settlers moved into what would become Texas, the Comanches found their targets were now closer than Mexico, and targets are what the Texans became. By the time Anglos were claiming the land, Comanches not only had horses and superb riding skills, they had guns. They were so rich from looting and ransoming kidnap victims, they could afford the best weaponry. And they turned it on the Texans, who were not prepared for the Comanches' military might. The Texas Rangers were formed as an attempt at militia-style control, but they were overwhelmed. The tribe raided so often and so viciously that, from the moment Anglos settled onto the land, everyone carried guns to protect themselves. They didn't have a choice. It wasn't until the Civil War was over and the U.S. Army fought the Comanches that the tide turned.

But despite the early conflicts, it was the Civil War that kicked Texas violence into high gear. Texas was a slave state but it wasn't very active in the Civil War as the Union Army blockaded the Mississippi River, separating Texas from the actual conflict. After the Civil War, however, Texas was in real trouble. That War armed and trained Southern men as it took their livelihoods away, and great gangs were formed that moved westward. Texas became a magnet for criminals. Any town without law enforcement was taken over by outlaw gangs. The gangs grew so powerful, they took over entire counties. They formed land mass chains through which rustled cattle and stolen horses were run and wanted criminals escaped. They obtained advanced weaponry and trained as armies. Vigilante groups formed to tame the lawlessness, and the result was huge numbers of lynchings, floggings, beatings, shootings— whatever the citizens felt was necessary to control the deluge of criminals. Many of the vigilante groups themselves became gangs and then warring mobs. The fighting between vigilante groups turned entire sections of the state into combat zones. Occasionally, the chaos was so intense that the U.S. Army declared martial law.

And on top of all that, the Ku Klux Klan operated in the state during and after the Civil War. Northern Texas had had a strong Union and abolitionist support base, and the Klan ripped through that area and lynched literally hundreds of white Unionists and Lincoln Republicans. The east central section of the state was cotton-growing land, and the Klan hit that area hard with its vicious lynchings of newly freed African Americans. Texas was pure anarchy and, in this maelstrom of violence, each vigilante group, each militia unit, each armed family was a law unto itself. The frontier mentality and the extraordinarily violent conditions of existence saw Texans picking up a gun whenever they saw a threat and carrying out whatever action they thought necessary. Survival in Texas was based on the willingness to use frontier justice.

Then, suddenly, it was over. The frontier was declared closed in the 1890 census, and vigilantism died with it. The last Indian War, the Battle of Wounded Knee, was fought in 1890 in South Dakota. Gold mines were mined out, and prospectors were gone. The open range was closed with barbed wire and horse and cattle rustling was stopped as homesteaders claimed the land. Territories became states, and with statehood came a whole new set of laws. With the advance of commerce, towns could afford police, jails, courthouses and prosecutors. Real law was brought to the West and improvisational law was outlawed. Americans had moved inexorably westward, ever settling the next piece of open and unclaimed land, and now that movement was done. There was no free land left. The West had been settled. Vigilantism was finished. Except when it wasn't.

CHAPTER 12

AND IN CONCLUSION

So when people ask, "Why is America so violent?", you need only look back at our history. We are a new nation, discovered relatively late in the history of the world. Early America was a Garden of Eden, a land so rich in natural resources a person could become wealthy in a short period of time. Europe was peopled with millions of peasants, the remnants of serfdom, living in dire poverty. In the Middle Ages, land had been the basis of wealth. America had 2 billion acres of land, much of it free. Europe's poor flooded the new American nation, desperate for land to feed their families. And America was a land without laws.

The farms were built long before the jails. There was no money for sheriffs. People had to protect themselves and they did, as best they could. This meant possession of guns.

The first economy was agricultural and the basis of the family farm was the horse. The theft of the horse meant the loss of the farm and, often, the family. Horse theft became quite lucrative and it was run by gangs. This was the first large-scale crime in America and it existed in every community. Farmers had to protect themselves and their livelihood, and so they formed gangs to counter the gangs stealing their horses. The gangs of farmers became known as vigilantes – they were groups of men who took the law into their own hands. Because vigilantism existed before sheriffs and jails and courts, vigilantism is considered the basis of early American law and order. America is the only country in history that has had a system of vigilantism.

But we're not settlers anymore, you say. Let me turn back to my own story and show you how close those settler days are to me. My grandfather was a child in the days before the frontier was declared closed in 1890. He was poor, and his family used their rifle to shoot dinner. Without the gun, they would have had very little food. The vigilante movement that broke the stranglehold German-Americans had on the Midwest occurred when my own parents were children. And when I was a child, a vigilante movement ran me and my very dangerous father out of town. Here I am, a senior citizen, a New Yorker, a Democrat, and look how my own life was defined by gun culture.

So when people ask, "Why is America so violent?," I say, "Look at our history." We began as a land without laws. Guns were basic to settler survival, and gun culture and its group manifestation, vigilantism, reigned. Guns and vigilantism are part of the American collective experience. We can't outrun our history. And making peace with a history as violent as ours is not an easy task.

CHAPTER 13
MY RESEARCH

As I have said, this is a personal story. The history contained herein is the history I studied to understand the vigilantism I experienced as a child. Much of the material in this book can be found by using Google. The most productive research on many of these topics was found on the university websites, those websites ending in .edu. Some of the best writing on American history is published on university websites as books and dissertations.

I will suggest some starting points in these books that I found valuable:

They Chose Minnesota: A Survey of the State's Ethnic Groups, by Michael Albert, Hyman Berman, edited by June Drenning Holmquist, Minnesota Historical Society Press (1981)

A series of essays that give concrete details on immigration and settlement

The Minds of the West: Ethnocultural Evolution in the Rural Middle West, 1830–1917, by Jon Gjerde, The University of North Carolina Press (February 10, 1999)

A study of German immigration and the German-America refusal to assimilate

The Tragedy of German-America (The American immigration collection, Series II), by John Arkas Hawgood, Ayer Co Pub (June 1970)

The definitive book on the German attempt to colonize the Midwest

Methland: The Death and Life of an American Small Town, by Nick Reding, Bloomsbury USA (June 9, 2009)

The story of the devastation of methamphetamine in Iowa

Strain of Violence: Historical Studies of American Violence and Vigilantism, by Richard Maxwell Brown, Oxford University Press, USA, First Edition (January 2, 1975)

A survey of American vigilantism

American Terrorist: Timothy McVeigh & The Oklahoma City Bombing, by Lou Michel and Dan Herbeck, HarperCollins (May 1, 2001)

A book by the two journalists who spent 75 hours interviewing McVeigh

Every Knee Shall Bow: The Truth & Tragedy of Ruby Ridge & The Randy Weaver Family, Jess Walter, HarperCollins (January 1, 1995)

A carefully written book about a very controversial situation

Columbine, by Dave Cullen, Twelve (April 6, 2009)

The award-winning account of the shooting at Columbine High School